Alfred's Basic Piano Library

Book Four

Y0-BOA-059

All-in-One Course
Lesson · Theory · Solo

FOREWORD

This All-in-One Piano Course was written in response to many requests by piano teachers for just one all encompassing teaching book, that would include LESSON, THEORY and SOLO material. By combining all the LESSON BOOKS of Levels 1A, 1B and 2 of Alfred's Basic Piano Library into five consecutive books (Books 1–5) that also include selected pages from the THEORY, RECITAL and FUN BOOKS, a new course has been developed that offers several advantages:

1. The student will need to perform from only one book. The need to carry multiple books to each lesson is eliminated.

2. Teacher assignments will be simplified, as the Lesson, Theory and Solo material are all combined in perfect sequence.

3. While less supplementary material is included than if the Theory, Recital and Fun Books were used individually, the same "overlapping concepts" used in the regular edition of Alfred's Basic Piano Library is continued.

4. At the completion of Book 4 of the All-in-One Course, the student will have completed all of the fundamentals covered in Levels 1A through the first half of Level 2 and will be ready to continue into Book 5 of the All-in-One Course.

Here is an outline of the basic contents of Book 4.

Pages 2, 3   Middle C Position & Middle D Position.
 4, 5   Review of musical terms.
 6–9   Dotted quarter notes.
 10–17   The interval of a 6th in C position. Changing time signatures.
 18–21   The interval of a 6th in G position.
 22–25   The interval of a 6th in C and G positions.
 26–29   Moving up & down the keyboard in 6ths. *mp*.
 30–41   Crossing RH 2 over 1. Crossing LH 2 over 1. *ff* & *pp*.
 42–47   The interval of a 7th.
 48   Diploma.

Illustrations by Christine Finn
Book production by Greg Plumblee and Linda Lusk

A General MIDI disk is available (14413), which includes a full piano recording and background accompaniment.

Willard A. Palmer • Morton Manus • Amanda Vick Lethco

Get Away!

This piece uses both the **MIDDLE C POSITION** and the **MIDDLE D POSITION.**

Adapted from themes from
the Overture to "William Tell,"
by G. Rossini

MIDDLE C POSITION

Identify the U.F.O.'s!

The U.F.O.'s (Unidentified Flying Objects) on pages 4 and 5 can be changed
to I.F.O.'s (Identified Flying Objects)!

To change the U.F.O.'s to I.F.O.'s, print the names of each space ship on the tag attached to it.
Select from the following names:

QUARTER REST	SHARP	FORTE	TIED NOTES	TIME SIGNATURE
HALF REST	FLAT	MEZZO FORTE	ACCENT	REPEAT
WHOLE REST	NATURAL	PIANO	FERMATA	EIGHTH NOTES

SCORE 100 FOR EACH U.F.O. YOU IDENTIFY! PERFECT SCORE IS 1,500!

FOR BONUS SCORE, ANSWER THE FOLLOWING QUESTIONS
TO MAKE 1,700 AND QUALIFY AS A SUPER-STUDENT!

1. *p–f* means _____ .

2. _____ means "gradually _____."

FINAL SCORE: _____

Introducing Dotted Quarter Notes

A DOT INCREASES THE LENGTH OF A NOTE BY ONE HALF ITS VALUE.

A **dotted half note** is equal to a half note tied to a quarter note.

$$\begin{array}{ccccc} 2 & + & 1 & = & 3 \\ \text{COUNTS} & & \text{COUNT} & & \text{COUNTS} \end{array}$$

A **dotted quarter note** is equal to a quarter note tied to an eighth note.

$$\begin{array}{ccccc} 1 & + & \frac{1}{2} & = & 1\frac{1}{2} \\ \text{COUNT} & & \text{COUNT} & & \text{COUNTS} \end{array}$$

Clap (or tap) the following rhythm. Clap **ONCE** for each note, counting aloud.

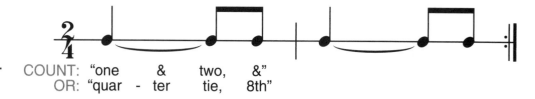

COUNT: "one   &   two,   &"
OR: "quar - ter   tie,   8th"

The only difference in the following two measures and those directly above them is the way they are written. They are played the same.

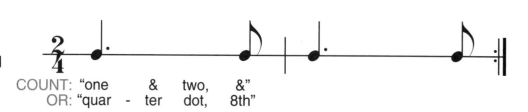

COUNT: "one   &   two,   &"
OR: "quar - ter   dot,   8th"

In $\frac{2}{4}$, $\frac{3}{4}$, or $\frac{4}{4}$ time, the DOTTED QUARTER NOTE is almost ALWAYS followed by an EIGHTH NOTE!

Alouette

C POSITION

Dotted Quarter Notes in $\frac{3}{4}$ Time

1. In the following line, draw TIES as indicated.
2. Play and count.
3. Play and sing the words.

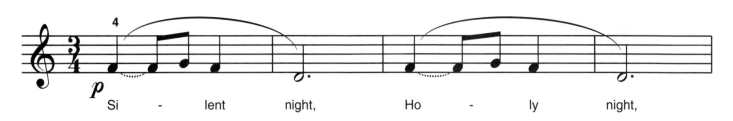

Si - lent   night,   Ho - ly   night,

4. In the following line, some quarter notes need dots.
   Add the correct dots to make the rhythm the same as above.
5. Play and count. This line should sound *exactly* the same as the one above.

Dotted Quarter Notes in $\frac{4}{4}$ Time

1. In the following line, draw TIES as indicated.
2. Play and count.
3. Play and sing the words.

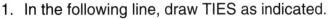

1. Sleep,   my child, and   peace   at - tend   thee,   All   through   the   night;
2. Guard - ian an - gels   God   will send   thee,   All   through   the   night.

4. In the following line, there are some dots missing from quarter notes and some flags missing from eighth notes. Add everything that is needed to make the rhythm the same as above.
5. Play and count. This line should sound *exactly* the same as the one above.

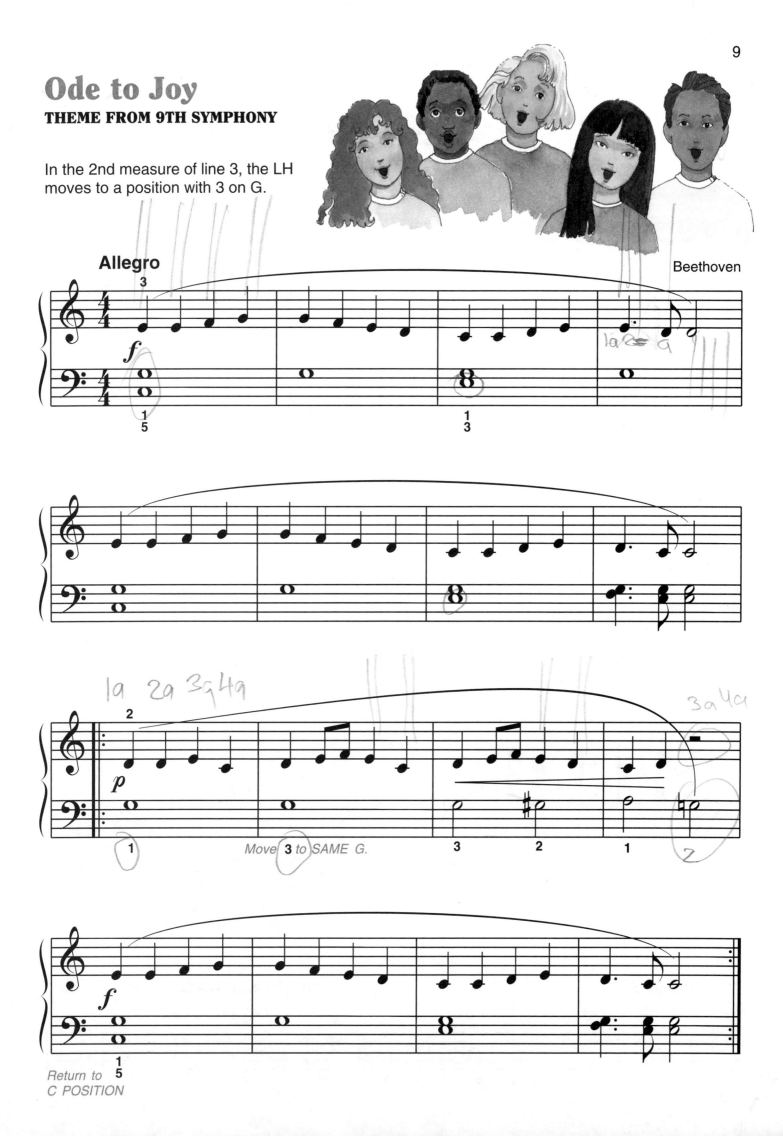

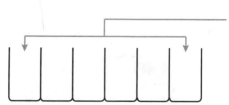

When you skip 4 white keys, the interval is a **6th**.

6ths are written LINE-SPACE or SPACE-LINE.

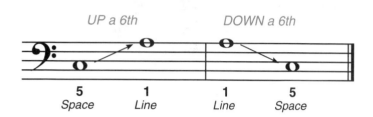

UP a 6th   DOWN a 6th

5   1   1   5
Space   Line   Line   Space

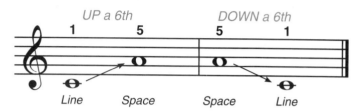

UP a 6th   DOWN a 6th

1   5   5   1
Line   Space   Space   Line

5 FINGERS can play 6 NOTES: C D E F G A

RH

This is C POSITION plus 1 note (A)
played with RH 5.

1 2 3 4 5 5

RH 5 plays G or A!

Say the names of these intervals as you play!

MELODIC INTERVALS:

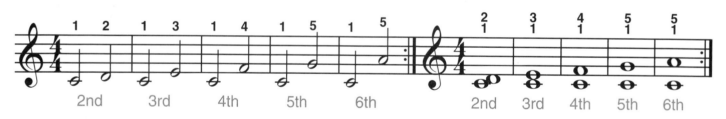

1 2   1 3   1 4   1 5   1 5

2nd   3rd   4th   5th   6th

HARMONIC INTERVALS:

2/1   3/1   4/1   5/1   5/1

2nd   3rd   4th   5th   6th

LH

This is C POSITION plus 1 note (A)
played with LH 1.

5 4 3 2 1 1

LH 1 plays G or A!

Say the names of these intervals as you play!

MELODIC INTERVALS:

2nd   3rd   4th   5th   6th

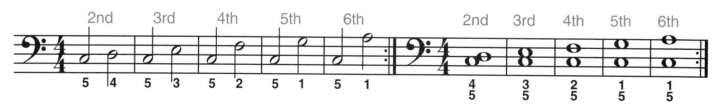

5 4   5 3   5 2   5 1   5 1

HARMONIC INTERVALS:

2nd   3rd   4th   5th   6th

4/5   3/5   2/5   1/5   1/5

Writing 6ths

Remember: 6ths are written LINE-SPACE or SPACE-LINE.

1. Write the name of each note in the following boxes.
2. Play these MELODIC INTERVALS, saying "Up a 6th," etc.

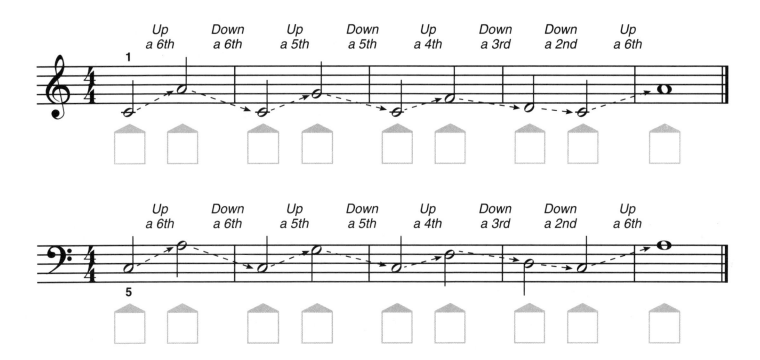

3. In each measure below, add a higher whole note to make the indicated HARMONIC INTERVAL.

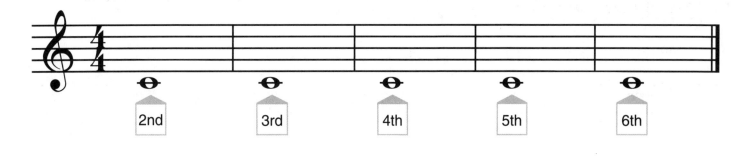

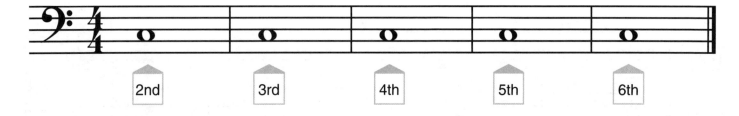

4. Play the above two lines. Use RH 1–5 or LH 5–1 on each 5th and 6th.

12

Practice this WARM-UP before playing LAVENDER'S BLUE.

Lavender's Blue

Allegro moderato

mf

Lav - en - der's blue, dil - ly, dil - ly, Lav - en - der's green.
Who told you so, dil - ly, dil - ly, Who told you so?

When I am King, dil - ly, dil - ly, You shall be Queen!
'Twas my own heart, dil - ly, dil - ly, That told me so!

p *ritardando*

SUGGESTION: For a WARM-UP, practice the first 4 measures with LH alone.

When You Grow Up

Willard A. Palmer

Allegro moderato

OPTIONAL: After playing the piece twice, repeat the last line slowly and softly with both hands *8va.*

QUESTION: What would you like to be? _____

(answer)

Interval Search

Draw a flight path from each beehive to the flower that contains the interval of the same name. The paths may cross, but may not pass through a different interval! (There will be two bees from each beehive.)

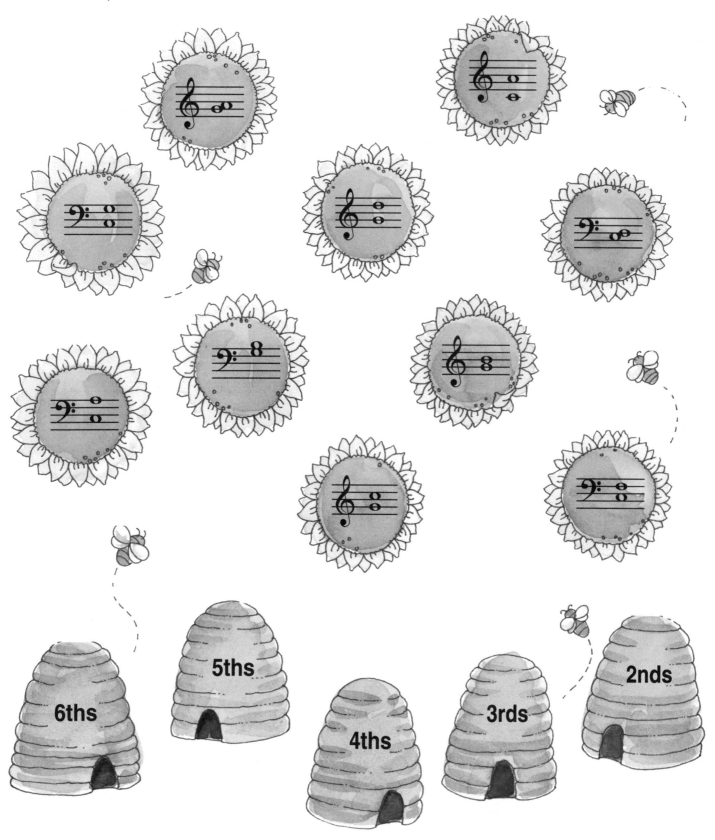

Score 10 for each interval found.

PERFECT SCORE = 100

YOUR SCORE _____

This piece uses 2/4 and 4/4 time,
changing time signatures in each measure.

COUNT: 1 - 2 | 1 - 2 - 3 - 4 | *etc.*

Kum-ba-yah!*

Andante
2nd time both hands 8va

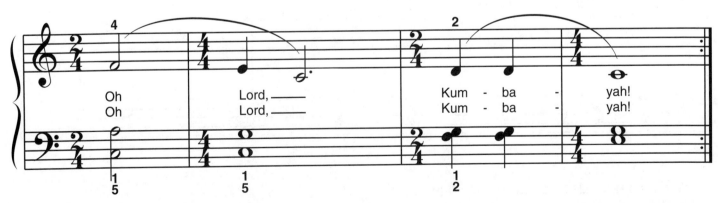

Kum-ba-yah means "Come by here."

Rockin' on 6!

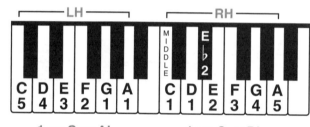

1 on G or A!

1 on C or D!
2 on E or E♭!

Moderate rock tempo

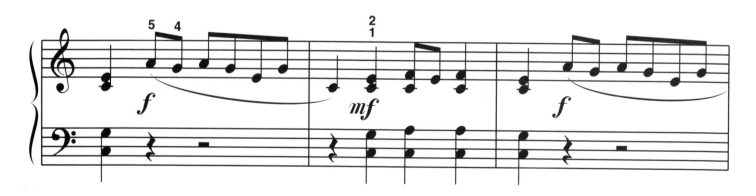

Rockin' on 6 may also be played with a jazz feel.
Pairs of eighth notes would be played a bit unevenly (long-short).

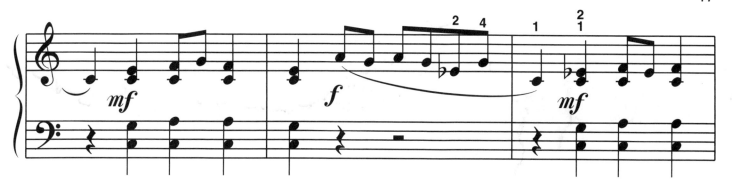

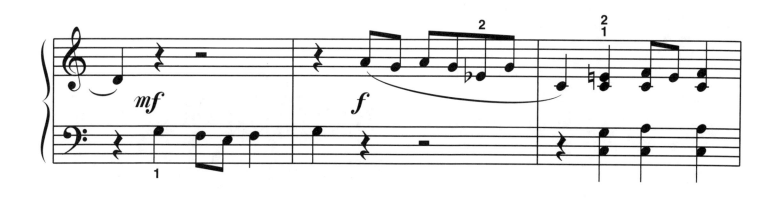

8va

Measuring 6ths in G Position

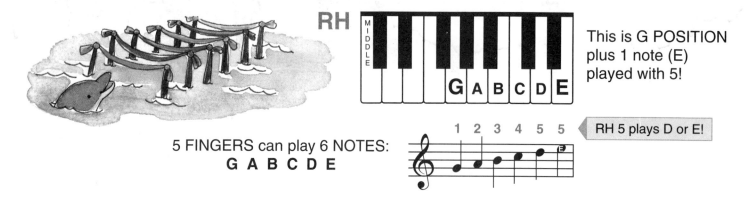

RH

This is G POSITION plus 1 note (E) played with 5!

5 FINGERS can play 6 NOTES:
G A B C D E

RH 5 plays D or E!

Say the names of the intervals as you play!

MELODIC INTERVALS:

HARMONIC INTERVALS:

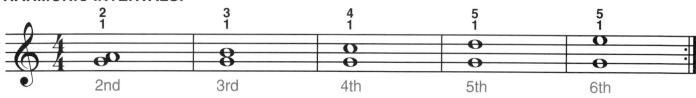

LH

This is G POSITION plus1 note (E) played with 1!

LH 1 plays D or E!

Say the names of the intervals as you play!

MELODIC INTERVALS:

HARMONIC INTERVALS:

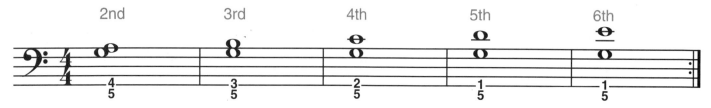

Writing 6ths in G Position

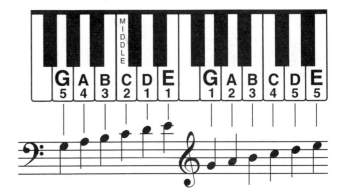

1. In each measure below, add one higher whole note to make the indicated HARMONIC interval.
2. Play. Use RH 1-5 on the 5th and the 6th.

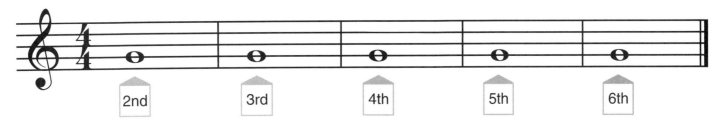

3. In each measure below, add one higher whole note to make the indicated HARMONIC interval.
4. Play. Use LH 5-1 on the 5th and the 6th.

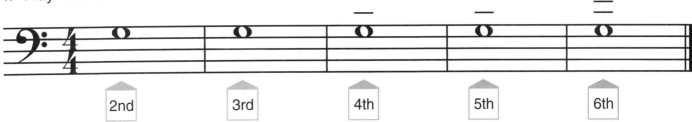

5. Write the name of each note in the following boxes.
6. Play, saying "Down a 4th," etc.

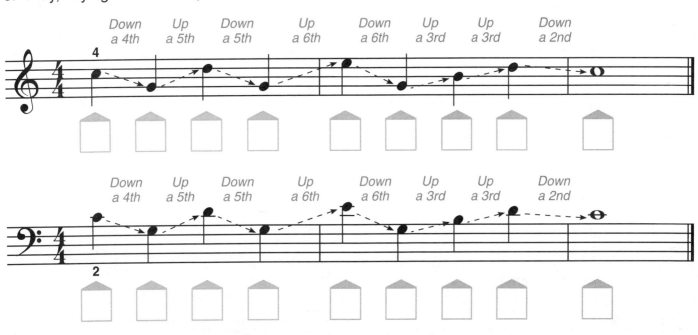

7. What kind of intervals (harmonic or melodic) did you play in the last 2 lines?_____

I'm Gonna Sing!

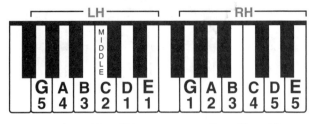

1 on D or E!   5 on D or E!

Spiritual

Allegro

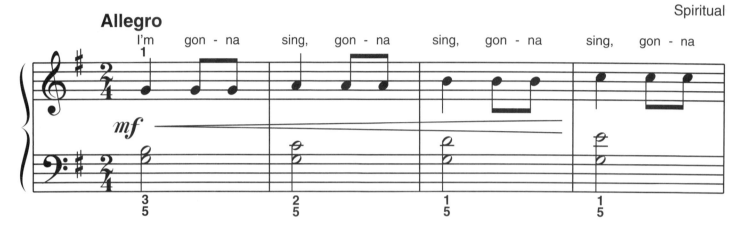

I'm gon - na sing, gon - na sing, gon - na sing, gon - na

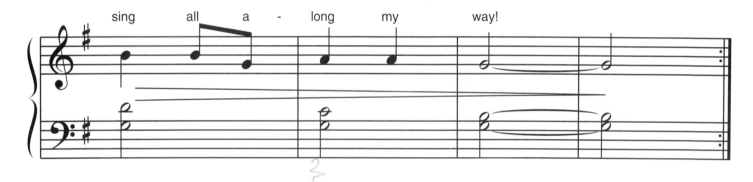

sing all a - long my way!

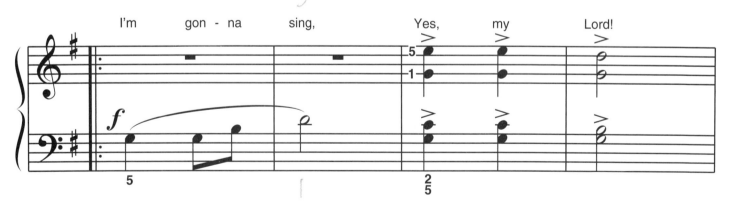

I'm gon - na sing, Yes, my Lord!

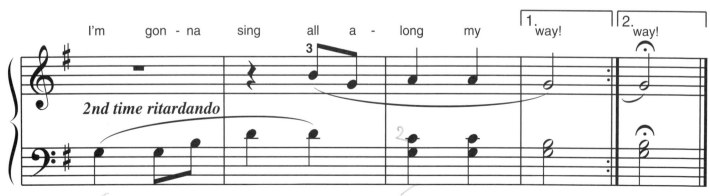

I'm gon - na sing all a - long my way! way!

2nd time ritardando

18th Century Dance

This piece uses the position shown on page 20.

Andante moderato

When you play in positions that include 6 or more notes, *any* finger may be required to play 2 notes.

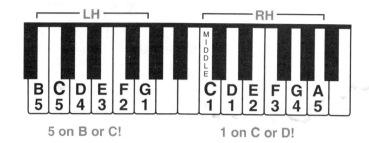

5 on B or C!   1 on C or D!

RH INTERVALS, from A down to C:

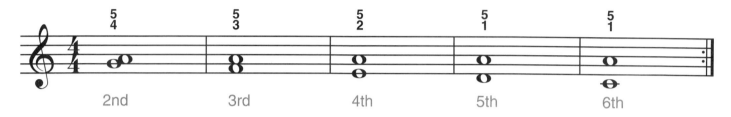

2nd   3rd   4th   5th   6th

LH INTERVALS, from G down to B:

2nd   3rd   4th   5th   6th

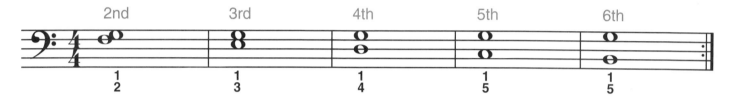

London Bridge

Allegro
2nd time play RH 8va

English Folk Song

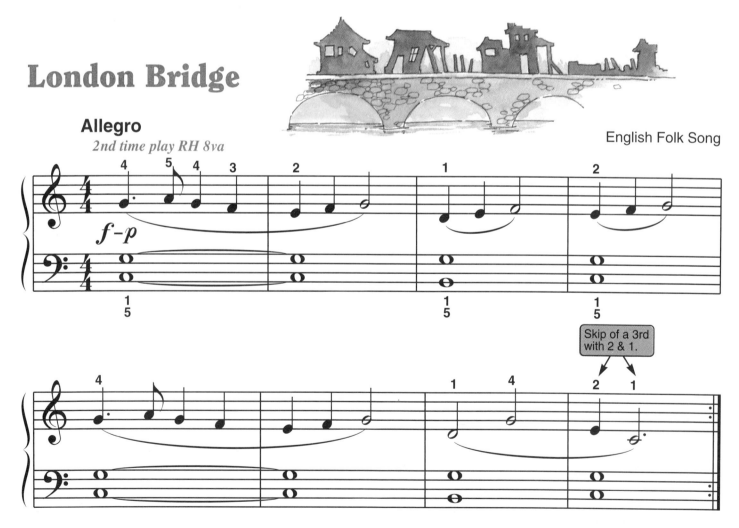

Skip of a 3rd with 2 & 1.

The original London bridge, about which this song was written, was in danger of falling down because it was covered with tall, rickety buildings. It was torn down and rebuilt after 1757.

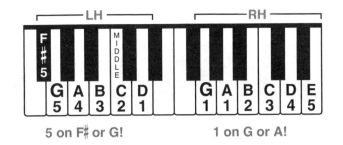

5 on F♯ or G!   **1 on G or A!**

RH INTERVALS, from E down to G:

LH INTERVALS, from D down to F♯:

Nick Nack Paddy Wack

(This Old Man)

Allegro moderato
2nd time play RH 8va

f–p

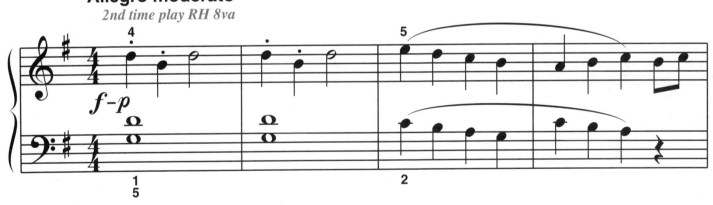

RH G POSITION

Wash-Day Boogie

Allegro moderato

mf

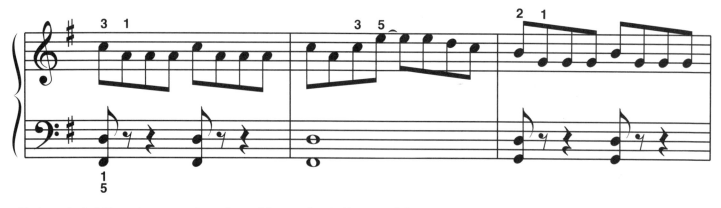

Pairs of eighth notes may be played long-short, if you wish.

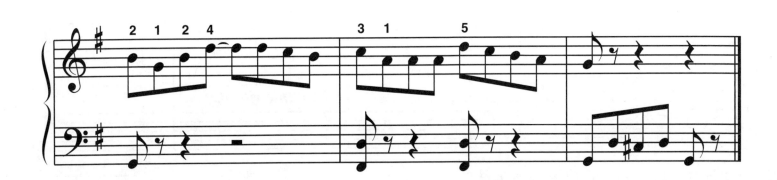

Moving Up & Down the Keyboard in 6ths

In the following exercises, the hands are no longer confined to one position!
Each hand plays 6ths, moving 1 and 5 up and down the keyboard to neighboring keys.

RH 6ths, MOVING FROM A C **UP TO** E G **AND BACK.**

Begin with RH 1 on MIDDLE C.

LH 6ths, MOVING FROM C E **DOWN TO** F A **AND BACK.**

Begin with LH 1 on MIDDLE C.

Lone Star Waltz

This piece combines the positions used in
LONDON BRIDGE (p. 22) with MOVING
UP & DOWN THE KEYBOARD IN 6ths.

Moderato
2nd time both hands 8va

Willard A. Palmer

2nd time ritard.

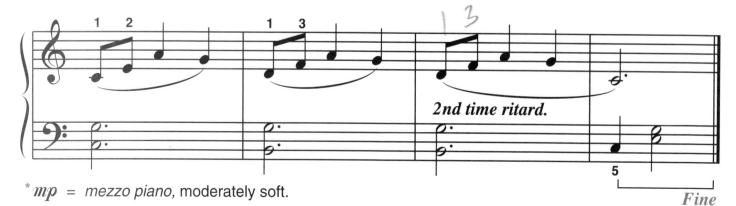

mp = mezzo piano, moderately soft.

Fine

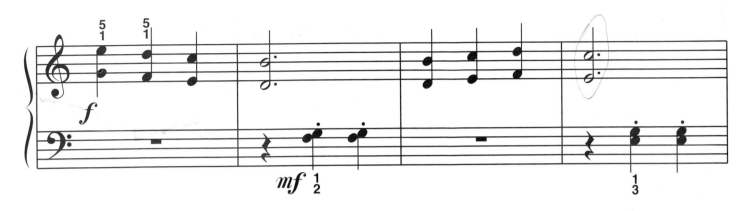

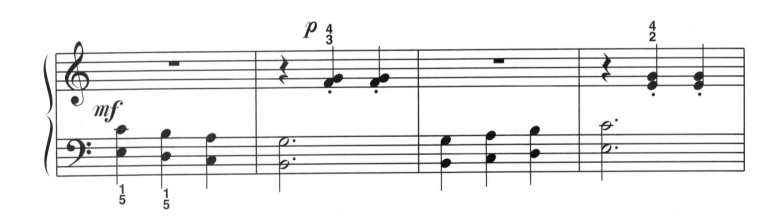

D. C. al Fine

Writing 6ths Up & Down the Keyboard

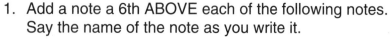

1. Add a note a 6th ABOVE each of the following notes.
   Say the name of the note as you write it.
2. Play, using RH 1–5 on each 6th.

3. Add a note a 6th BELOW each of the following notes.
   Say the name of the note as you write it.
4. Play, using LH 5–1 on each 6th.

5. Play the two lines as one complete piece—play RH, then LH.

Writing 6ths Around the Keyboard

1. Add a note a 6th ABOVE each of the following notes.
   Say the name of the note as you write it.
2. Play, using RH 1–5 on each 6th.

3. Add a note a 6th BELOW each of the following notes.
   Say the name of the note as you write it.
4. Play, using LH 5–1 on each 6th.

5. Play the two lines as one complete piece—play RH, then LH.

Listen to the Mocking Bird

Alice Hawthorne

Andante moderato

Lis - ten to the mock - ing bird, Lis - ten to the mock - ing bird,

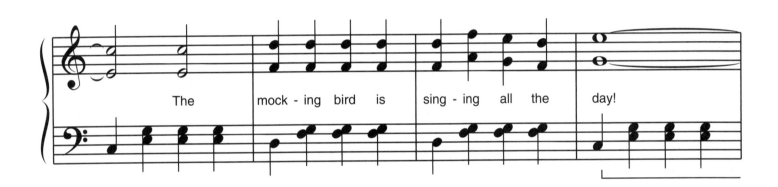

The mock - ing bird is sing - ing all the day!

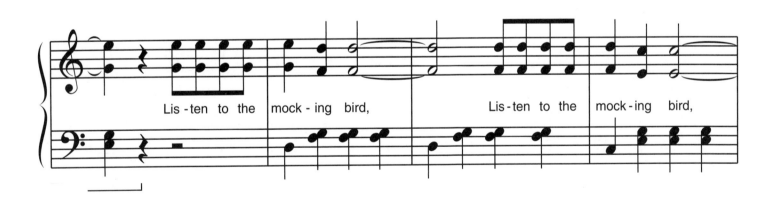

Lis - ten to the mock - ing bird, Lis - ten to the mock - ing bird,

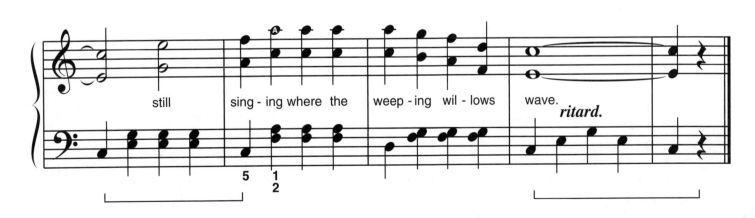

still sing - ing where the weep - ing wil - lows wave. *ritard.*

Crossing RH 2 over 1

In this exercise, each phrase begins with a new hand position, one key LOWER than the one before.

Begin the first phrase with 5 on F,
the second phrase with 5 on E,
the third phrase with 5 on D, etc.

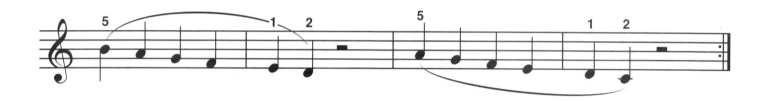

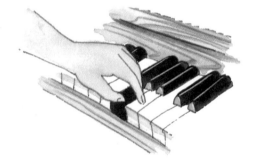

Crossing LH 2 over 1

In this exercise, each phrase begins with a new hand position, one key HIGHER than the one before.

Begin the first phrase with 5 on G,
the second phrase with 5 on A,
the third phrase with 5 on B, etc.

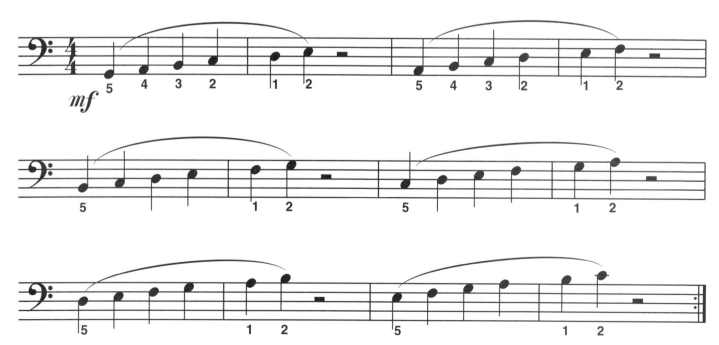

On the Bridge at Avignon
(SUR LE PONT D'AVIGNON)

French Folk Song

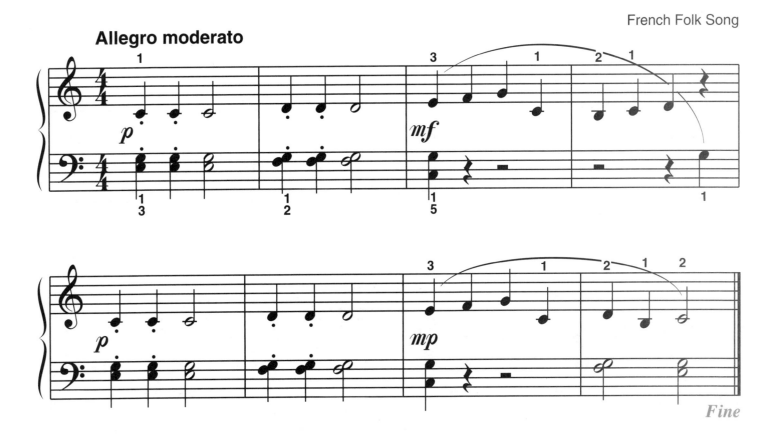

This is a song about another rickety bridge, a very wide one, located in the city of Avignon, in France. Legend has it that so many people once danced on this bridge that it almost collapsed.

Come, Thou Almighty King

Felice de Giardini

Andante moderato

Come, Thou al - might - y King, Help us Thy

name to sing, Help us to praise! Fa - ther all -

glo - ri - ous, O'er all vic - to - ri - ous, Come and reign

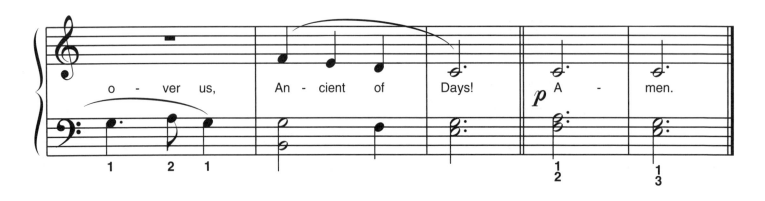

o - ver us, An - cient of Days! A - men.

Figuring the Fingering

Now that you have learned the trick of crossing 2 over 1 and are becoming more skilled at moving to different positions on the keyboard, you can begin to choose your own fingering.

1. Fill in the squares with the best finger numbers for playing this piece. The first finger for each line is given. Notice that you do not have to finger every note. The second measure of each line is exactly like the first; it is played with the same fingering.

2. Play the piece several times, using the fingering you wrote.

Ragtime Man

Fine

D. C. al Fine

Malagueña

Malagueña, pronounced "mah-lah-GAIN-yah," is a title given to certain types of Spanish dances and songs composed or improvised in a style that originated in the Spanish region of Málaga.

There are many *malagueñas,* just as there are many *tangos* and *waltzes.* The melody divided between the hands at the beginning and end of this piece, as well as the descending LH and RH patterns in the middle sections, are characteristic of the style.

In this piece the LH begins in TREBLE CLEF. In measures 7–9, 27–29 and 31–33, the RH plays in BASS CLEF.

NEW DYNAMIC SIGNS

ff *(fortissimo)*
means VERY LOUD.

pp *(pianissimo)*
means VERY SOFT.

Allegro moderato

Spanish Folk Melodies

REVIEW: Six Dynamic Signs

p	pp	f	ff	mp	mf

1. Each of the above dynamic signs has two matches below;
   one in the LEFT column and one in the RIGHT column.

   Draw each sign TWICE; once in a square in the LEFT column and
   once in a square in the RIGHT column.

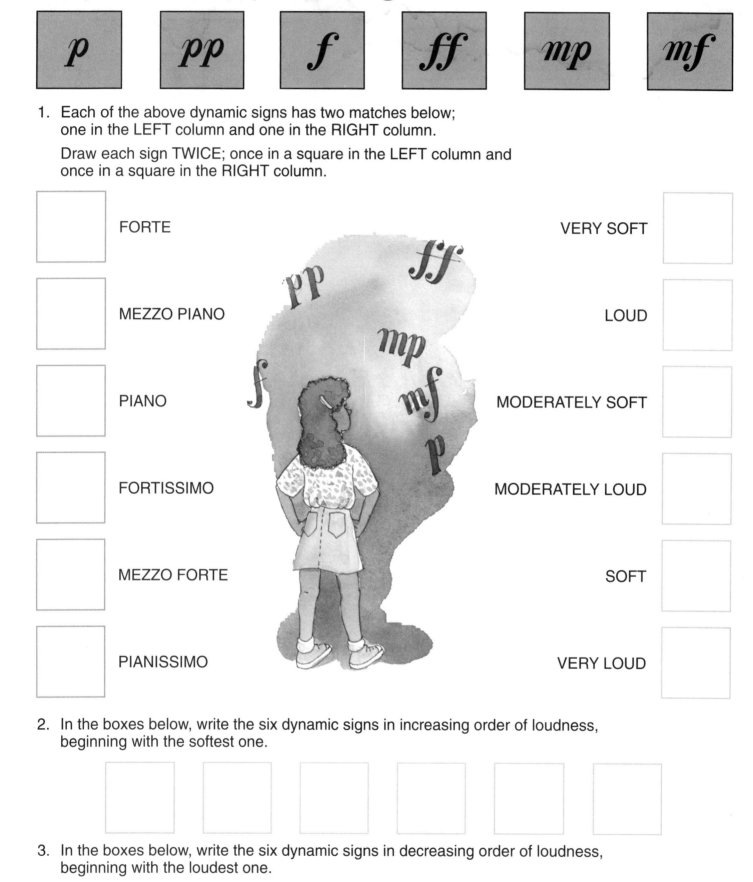

	LEFT		RIGHT	
☐	FORTE	VERY SOFT	☐
☐	MEZZO PIANO	LOUD	☐
☐	PIANO	MODERATELY SOFT	☐
☐	FORTISSIMO	MODERATELY LOUD	☐
☐	MEZZO FORTE	SOFT	☐
☐	PIANISSIMO	VERY LOUD	☐

2. In the boxes below, write the six dynamic signs in increasing order of loudness,
   beginning with the softest one.

   ☐ ☐ ☐ ☐ ☐ ☐

3. In the boxes below, write the six dynamic signs in decreasing order of loudness,
   beginning with the loudest one.

   ☐ ☐ ☐ ☐ ☐ ☐

Score 5 for each box correctly filled.

PERFECT SCORE = 120   YOUR SCORE _____

The Musical Private Eye

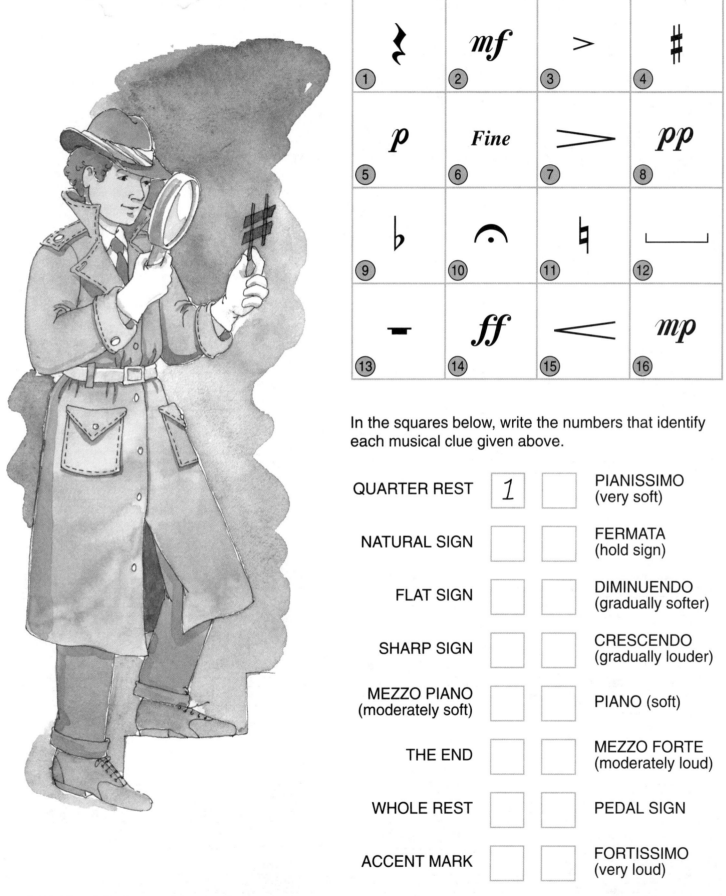

In the squares below, write the numbers that identify each musical clue given above.

QUARTER REST	*1*		PIANISSIMO (very soft)
NATURAL SIGN			FERMATA (hold sign)
FLAT SIGN			DIMINUENDO (gradually softer)
SHARP SIGN			CRESCENDO (gradually louder)
MEZZO PIANO (moderately soft)			PIANO (soft)
THE END			MEZZO FORTE (moderately loud)
WHOLE REST			PEDAL SIGN
ACCENT MARK			FORTISSIMO (very loud)

Add 10 points for each correct answer.
A perfect score is 150!

SCORE _____

Evening Song

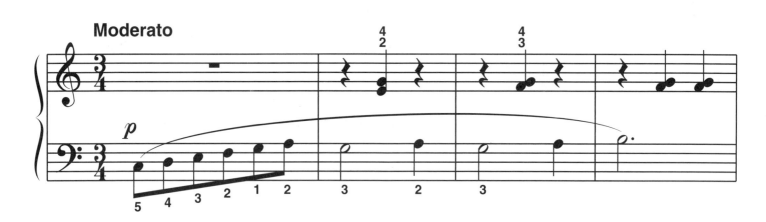

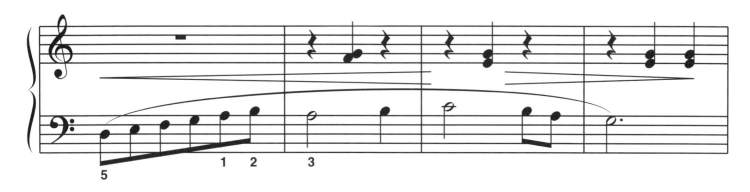

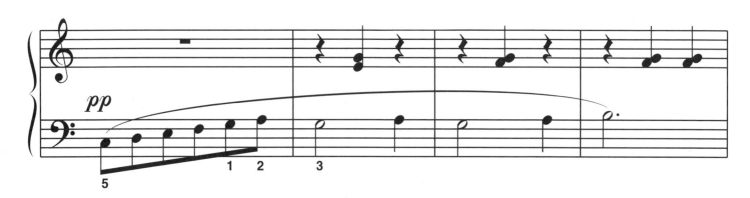

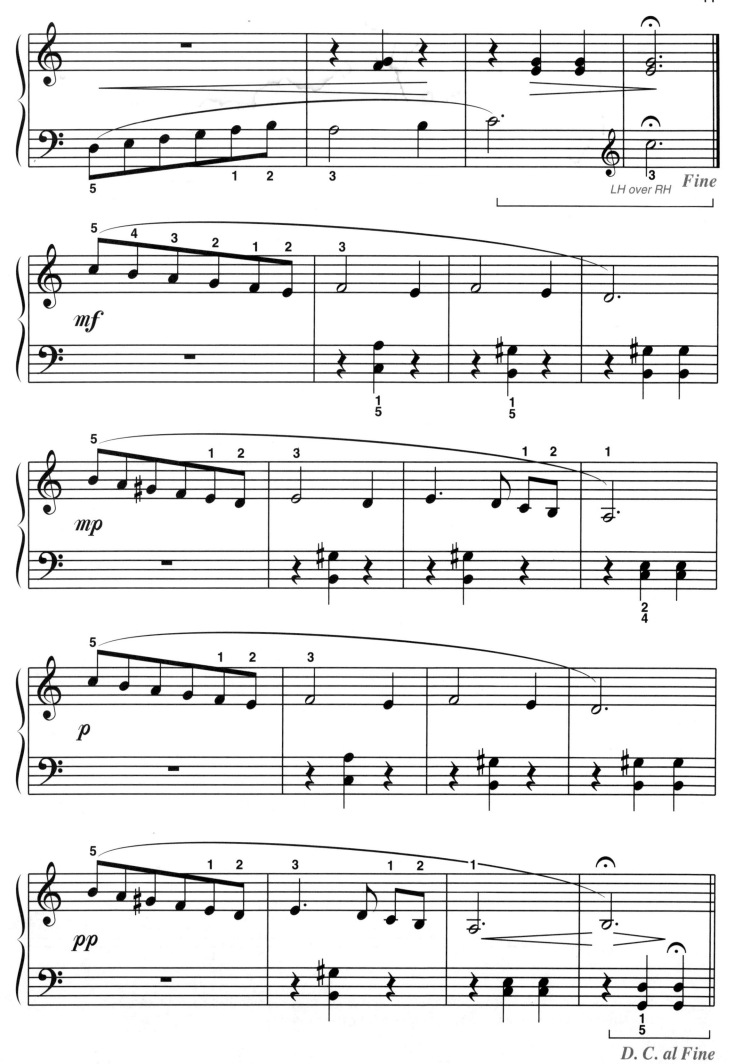

LH over RH   *Fine*

D. C. al Fine

42

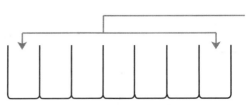

When you skip 5 white keys, the interval is a **7th.**

7ths are written LINE-LINE or SPACE-SPACE.

RH MELODIC INTERVALS:

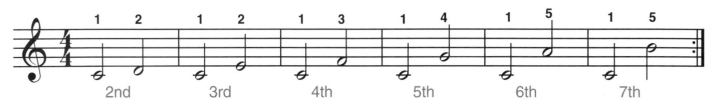

7ths (beginning on middle C):

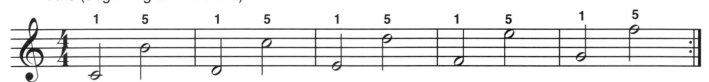

LH MELODIC INTERVALS:

7ths (beginning on low G):

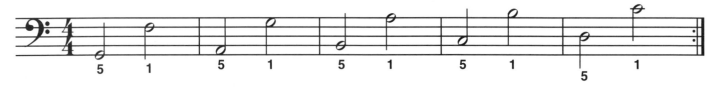

NOTE: Students with hands large enough to reach a 7th may repeat the above exercises, playing all the intervals harmonically (both notes together).

Writing 7ths

Remember: 7ths are written LINE-LINE or SPACE-SPACE.

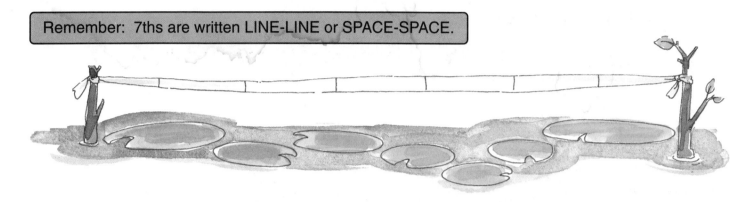

1. In each measure below, add a higher half note to make the indicated MELODIC interval.

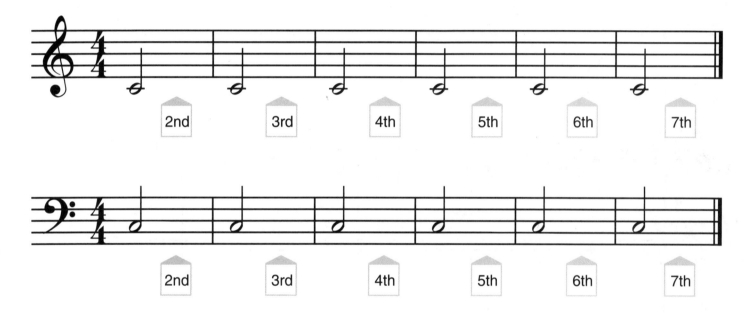

2. Play the above two lines. Use RH 1–5 on the 6th & 7th. Use LH 5–1 on the 5th, 6th & 7th.

3. Above each of the following notes write another whole note to make a HARMONIC 7th.

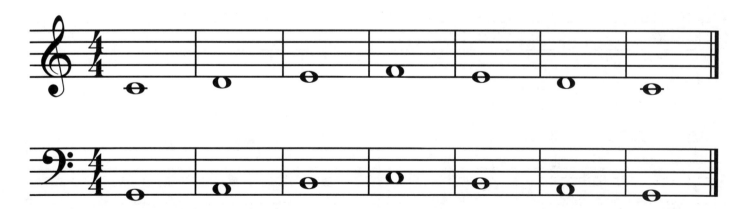

4. Play. Use RH 1–5 or LH 5–1 on each 7th.
   Students with hands too small to reach a 7th may divide each of the above lines between the hands, playing the bottom notes of the 7ths with LH 3, and the top notes with RH 3.

Our Special Waltz

Moderato

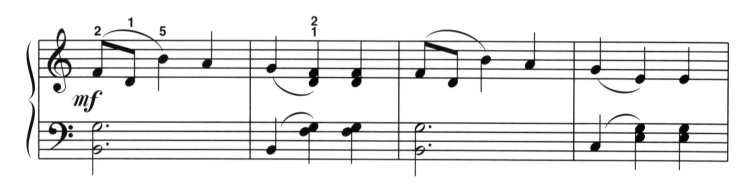

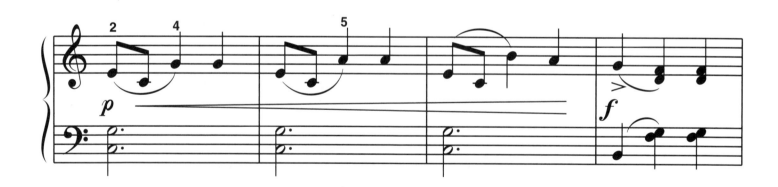

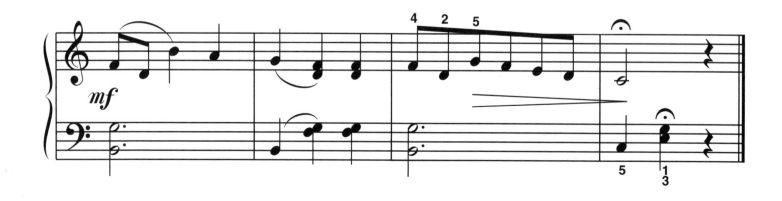

"Lucky Seven" Polka

1. In the music below, circle each pair of notes that make a MELODIC 7th.
2. How many harmonic 2nds can you find?   *(Answer)* _____
3. How many harmonic 3rds? _____
4. Harmonic 4ths? _____
5. Harmonic 5ths? _____
6. Harmonic 6ths? _____
7. Harmonic 7ths? _____

Clementine

American Folk Tune

Andante moderato

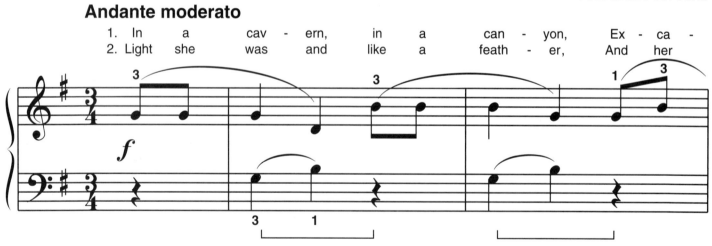

1. In a cav - ern, in a can - yon, Ex - ca -
2. Light she was and like a feath - er, And her

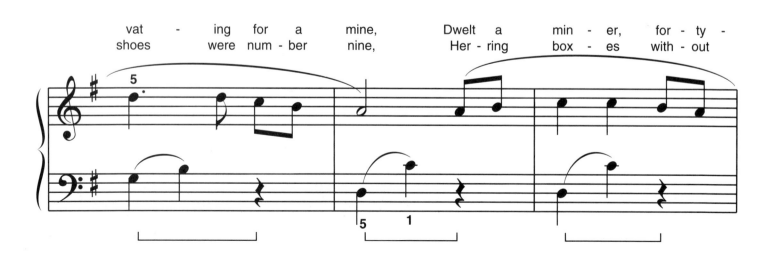

vat - ing for a mine, Dwelt a min - er, for - ty -
shoes were num - ber nine, Her - ring box - es with - out

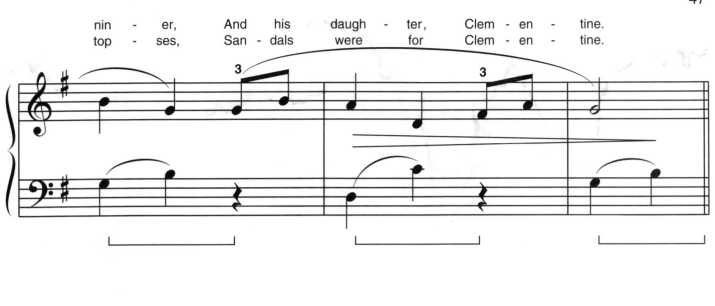

nin - er, And his daugh - ter, Clem - en - tine.
top - ses, San - dals were for Clem - en - tine.

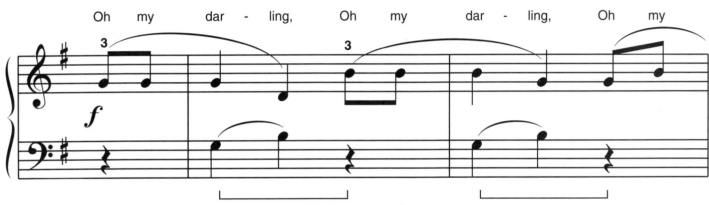

Oh my dar - ling, Oh my dar - ling, Oh my

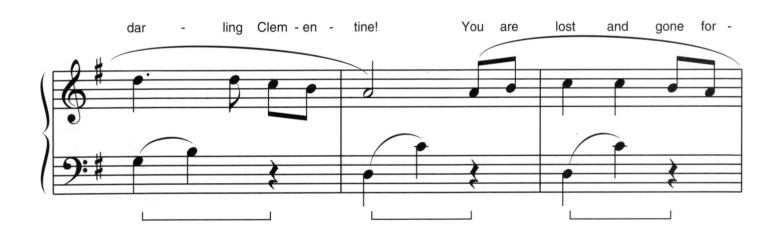

dar - ling Clem - en - tine! You are lost and gone for -

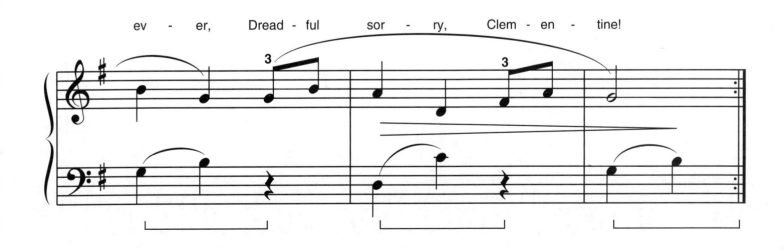

ev - er, Dread - ful sor - ry, Clem - en - tine!

Certificate of Promotion

This is to certify that

_____

has successfully completed the
All-in-One Course, Book 4
and is hereby promoted to the
All-in-One Course, Book 5.

Date _____

Teacher _____